REDIGGING THE WELLS OF OUR SPIRITUAL FOREFATHERS

by Tim Ranyak

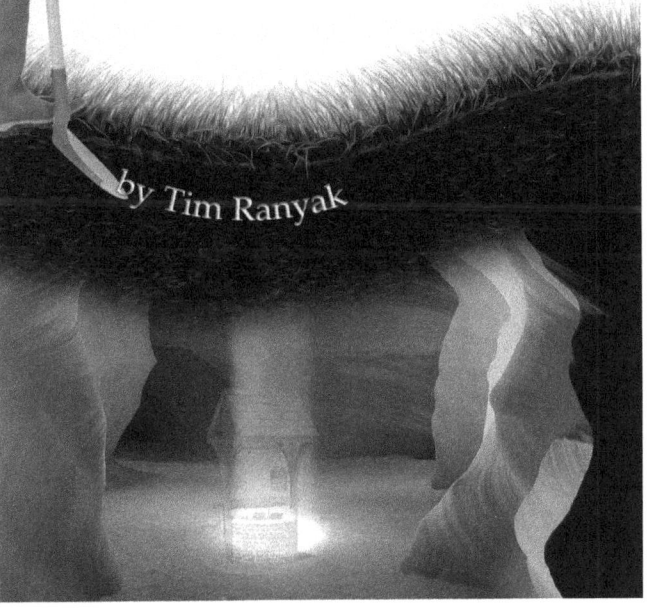

COPYRIGHT

Tim Ranyak
Re-Digging the Wells of Our Spiritual Forefathers

© 2013, Tim Ranyak
Self publishing
(www.revivalfireapostolic.org)

ALL RIGHTS RESERVED. This book contains material protected under International and Federal Copyright Laws and Treaties. Any unauthorized reprint or use of this material is prohibited. No part of this book may be reproduced or transmitted in any form or by any means, electronic or mechanical, including photocopying, recording, or by any information storage and retrieval system without express written permission from the author / publisher.

References:
- All scripture texts taken from KJV version of the Bible.
- Smith Wigglesworth referenced from Wikipedia Online
- All Greek and Hebrew words were taken from Strong's Exhaustive Concordance.

ISBN-10:
0-9891579-2-X
ISBN-13:
978-0-9891579-2-6

Publisher: Anointed Fire™

Book Dedication & Acknowledgments:

I would like to dedicate this book to all the men and women of God that suffer persecution for boldly proclaiming the Word of the Lord. For every minister, every missionary, and every soldier in and through Christ Jesus that is devoted to being part of that remnant. To every leader that will shake this nation, and the nations around the world for the God of all creation, Jesus Christ.

I would like to thank the God of my life Jesus Christ, Father God, and the Holy Spirit for moving upon me, through me, and inspiring me to write this book. I want to encourage all to use this for study materials as well in your church fellowships and groups as the Word of God has life giving power in it.

I would also like to thank my wife Cathie, my son Isaac, my daughters Hannah and Selah for their love and support of me. They are truly my best friends here on Earth, and they bring so much joy and love to my life. God Bless you all and may the God of peace that surpasses all understanding guard your hearts and minds, in and through Christ Jesus.

I would also like to thank all of my prayer warriors and intercessors. God is using you mightily as you pray for me. Multitudes upon multitudes of people will read these writings and will have the chance to be drawn closer to the Lord, and I pray that it is noted to your account as well as in Heaven. May the God of Glory fill you, keep you, and continue to inspire you; giving unto you the spirit of wisdom, knowledge, and revelation as you passionately pursue Him in all that you do.

And lastly, I would like to thank my mother Doris Ranyak, who rocked me in her arms, singing the gospel songs and hymns of the past over me, and releasing the presence of God in my life. Mom, you are a true warrior for Christ Jesus, and it is evident His hand has been upon you through thick and through thin. God has, and will always will be on your side because you choose to stand up for righteousness. May the God of peace grant you favor, wisdom, boldness and extended peace as you grow old, and may your latter end be greater than the former. I thank God for you. You are a true blessing to all who comes in contact with you. God Bless you richly.

Table of Contents

Introduction..viiii

Chapter 1: Digging......................................1

Chapter 2: Waiting For the Promise of the Father...7

Chapter 3: Pit-bull Tenacity....................................13

Chapter 4: The Battlefield..19

Chapter 5: Purging..23

Chapter 6: Walking in the Promise........................29

Chapter 7: Pursuing...35

Chapter 8: The Past is Over....................................39

Chapter 9: Faith Established..................................45

Chapter 10: Revival for the Fittest.........................53

Chapter 11: Signs and Wonders.............................67

Chapter 12: It Is Our Time To Shine......................75

Introduction

<u>Re-digging the Wells of Our Spiritual Forefathers</u> is a book based on a prophetic word the Holy Spirit shared with me. As we look at the times and the seasons which we are in, we see how men and women, children, and youth are hungry. Hungry for change. Hungry for something more. Hungry for something new!

What I am about to share is facts based on Biblical truths on how we really do not need something new; we need a refreshing touch from the Holy Spirit. We need God to breathe His fresh breath of life on us and the church once again. Perhaps, this may be the last time. Could it be that God is preparing to release unto us the greatest outpouring that the world has ever seen? Mark 16:17-18 declares: *"And these signs shall follow them that believe; In my name shall they cast out devils; they shall speak with new tongues; They shall take up serpents; and if they drink any deadly thing, it shall not hurt them; they shall lay hands on the sick, and they shall recover."*

The next verse of scripture I want to base this revelation on is Acts 1:8: *"But ye shall receive power, after that the Holy Ghost is come upon you: and ye shall be witnesses unto me both in Jerusalem, and in Judea, and in Samaria, and unto the uttermost part of the earth."*

And the third verse is found in John 14:12, which declares: *"Verily, verily. I say unto you, He that believeth on me, the works that I do shall he do also; and greater works than these shall he do; because I go unto my Father."*

Go with me as we search the pages of the most powerful book known to man, the Holy Bible, and let's get empowered as we scan back through time to see that Jesus Christ truly is the same, yesterday, today, and forever.

Chapter 1: Digging

As I scan through chapters and books of the pages of the Holy Bible, I can't help but notice one thing: Whether it was God in the Old Testament or Jesus in the New Testament, everything that was done by the hand of God was supernatural. From speaking "Let there be light," to framing the borders of the earth, everything was a supernatural work done by a supernatural God with supernatural wisdom.

Many get skiddish and even squirm in their chairs when they hear the word "supernatural" used in the church. Supernatural is not a common word to use in modern-day church gatherings. But in the days of God's Prophets; from John the Baptist to Jesus Christ's walk in the earth, we cannot help but see the term "supernatural" was just a common term for those who truly followed God.

Psalms 1 declares that everything we touch shall prosper, so shall it be for us that are true followers of Jesus Christ, as we are carriers of God's glory here in the earth. We have been set apart for such a time as this to be proclaimers of God's glorious truths, and carriers of the mantle of Jesus Christ. We have been called to fulfill the assignment that Jesus began here on the earth.

When Jesus started His ministry at age thirty-three, no one probably ever imagined how the world and society would be turned upside down as it was. Two thousand years ago, when laws were being established, out came one to bring change and transition for the people; a young zealous man for God coming to town, raising the dead, and restoring sight to the blind, in addition to all the other miracles Jesus did. Face it; it was unheard of, and the religious councils were not about to put up with it! It was not their culture; it was not their nature; it was not in the books of their laws, and surely He was not the ordinary religious leader they were accustomed to.

God had a creative plan that would flip the world upside down and set on course an irreversible mandate that would draw all men unto Himself.

Did man think that God was going to let the devil have his way forever? God knew exactly what was going to play out, and how it was going to play out as He stood looking over the sapphire hills of Heaven's gates, and declared into the air and space for Earth to exist. How sweet those words must have been had there been a man around to hear them. When He created you, formed you, and knitted you inside your mother's womb; He spoke with the same creative voice: "Harry, Bob, Bill, Margaret...Live!!!"

God is so creative in nature that mind cannot even

comprehend the things that God can even imagine. Our smartest and wisest thought is foolishness unto God. *"The foolishness of God is wiser than men; and the weakness of God is stronger than men" (1 Corinthians 1:25).*

If God did sleep, just from His breath alone would be enough creative power to frame another Earth. This is just how real and how powerful our God in Heaven is.

It is time to believe. Wake up sleepers. Romans 13:11-12 declares: *"And that, knowing the time, that now it is high time to awake out of sleep: for now is our salvation nearer than when we believed. The night is far spent, the day is at hand: let us therefore cast off the works of darkness, and let us put on the armor of light."*

1 Thessalonians 5:5-8 declares: *"Ye are all the children of the light, and the children of the day: we are not of the night, nor of darkness. Therefore let us not sleep, as do others; but let us watch and be sober. For they that sleep, sleep in the night; and they that be drunken, are drunken in the night. But let us, who are of the day, be sober, putting on the breastplate of faith and love; and for an helmet, the hope of salvation."*

Ephesians 5:14-17: *"Wherefore he saith, awake thou that sleepest, and arise from the dead, and Christ shall give thee light. See then that ye walk circumspectly, not as fools, but as wise, redeeming the time, because the days are evil. Wherefore be ye not unwise, but understanding what the will of the Lord is."*

I shared all of those verses to say this: God is saying in this hour to wake up!

Wake up to the fact that He is God, and we are not. Wake up to the fact that He has all power, and man does not. Wake up to the fact that all things belong unto God, including the earth and the world. Because the Word of God says: *"The Earth is the Lord's and the fullness thereof; the world, and they that dwell therein"* (Psalm 24:1). Psalm 50:10-12 declares: *"For every beast of the field is mine, and the cattle upon a thousand hills. I know all the fowls of the mountains: and the wild beasts of the field are mine. If I were hungry, I would not tell thee: for the world is mine, and the fullness thereof."* As we can see, God has created it all so therefore it all belongs unto God. *"God hath spoken once; twice have I heard this; that power belongeth unto God. Also unto thee O Lord, belongeth mercy: for thou renderest to every man according to his work"* (Psalm 62:11-12).

Our God is all powerful, all knowing, omnipresent, omniscient, and everlasting. Our Heavenly Father is eternal, everlasting, steadfast, and the wisdom behind wisdom. He is grace behind grace, and mercy behind mercy. God is love behind love, and He is our healer, deliverer, miracle worker, and coming King! God is the greatest wonder worker of all, and that will ever be. And the greatest thing of it all is: we are His. And as the scripture says, He is in us, and we are in Him!

John 1:1-5 states: *"In the beginning was the Word, and the Word was with God, and the Word was God. The same was in the beginning with God. All things were made by him; and without him was not anything made that was made. In Him was life; and the life was the light of men. And the light shineth in darkness; and the darkness comprehended it not."* The most awesome and the greatest thing about this passage is there is a great promise in it. 1 John states that He is in us, and we are in Him. That means we can interpret John 1:1 as: Jesus being the Word, as the Word lives in us and we in the Word.

RE-DIGGING THE WELLS OF OUR SPIRITUAL FOREFATHERS

Chapter 2: Waiting For the Promise of the Father

One of the most crucial things about digging wells is patience. Just like the disciples before they entered into the realm or sphere of operating in the supernatural, they waited on the promise of the Father. We too must wait on the promise of the Father. Before any of us are going to operate in the fullness that God has for us, we must understand two things: First, we are to be sure of our calling and elections. And second, we need to understand God's timing and positioning.

If we are sure of what God has called us to do, that means we now are unmovable, unshakable, and we cannot be talked out of who we are in Christ. Look at the Apostle Paul. If you look at the beginning of Paul's letters to the different churches, you will find that some start out with Paul the Apostle called by the will of God, some start with Paul called by the commandment of God, and others start out by saying Paul is being called by the will of God and not of man. And we all know that what the Apostle Paul accomplished, he accomplished it by the spirit and power of God and God alone. Likewise, this is true for each of us. For us to do and accomplish what it is God is calling us to do; we must be certain that God has ordained and graced us with the power that we need to get the job done. As we already saw in Acts 1:8, God has given us power by His Holy Spirit. That word "power" is the Greek word "dunamis," which translates to miracle working, wonder working power. It also means power, strength, violence, force. Reference this verse with Matthew 11:12, which declares: *"And from the days of John the Baptist until now the kingdom of Heaven suffereth violence, and the violent take it by force."* The word "violence" here is the word "biastes" which translates: a forcer, energetic, violent.

God has given us a power that lies way down deep in our spirits that many of us are totally unaware of. There are wells even in our spirit man that we have not even tapped into. These are wells of wealth, wisdom, strategy, power, consistency, and perseverance. God has equipped us with everything that we need to get the job done. Have you ever noticed when you get yourself in a pinch or in a tight position in life that under the pressure of it all, a creative idea comes forth all of a sudden? The idea was already inside the heart of your spirit, but your situation had to put a demand on that wealth of knowledge before you could obtain it.

The other thing I wanted to mention and explain is the importance of being in God's divine timing and positioning, both spiritually and geographically.

If the blind beggar had not been where he was at the passing by of Jesus, he would not have been healed. Had the Apostle Paul not been at the spot on the Damascus road, he may not have encountered Jesus. Had the pool of Bethesda not had any water in it for the angels to come down and stir, the souls that got in it would not have been healed. We are living in the hour and time where we must pay attention to the elements. Kingdom elements. The Bible declares that *"wisdom crieth without; she uttereth her voice in the streets"* (Proverbs 1:20). We must be attentive and alert to what is going on around us both spiritually and physically; in the spirit realm and in the natural realms.

In addition, there is the factor of being in the proper geographical location. Had Joseph the earthly father of Jesus not fled the region they were in, Jesus could have been killed before God's divine timing. Herod had put a contract out on all male babies at that time because he heard there was another king who had come, and he was fearful this king would take his place. Baby killing and seed stealing is not just in our culture; it has been around since the beginning of time, as have men fighting over thrones. Herod had such a devious, lustful, idolatrous spirit that he was willing to slaughter innocent lives for the sake of His own pleasure and gratification. Again look at the elements that are at work around us. This is a word for the hour in which we live.

Geographical timing and positioning are very critical elements that need to be in place, as well as being sure of our calling and election. This process can get demanding and cause many to give up.

No one ever said digging wells, or even re-digging wells was going to be an easy task. When Jacob found some of his father Abraham's wells and came to re-dig them, I am more than certain it was more than what he bargained for, and more than he wanted to bite off and chew.

A mighty move of God is coming to the Earth, but if we do not get back to holiness, repentance, and humility; we will never see the greater outpouring. When it comes to digging some stuff up, we all know that with it can come both the good and the bad.

Yes, especially when it comes to finding our gifts. What will constantly pop up in your mind is the voice of someone who said you can't, the voice of someone who said you won't, and the voice of someone who said you should not. We must rid ourselves of these negative mindsets and ask God to cleanse our hearts and minds as His Word declares that we have the mind of Christ. (See 1 Corinthians 2:16).

Re-digging wells is not a comfortable task, a cup of

tea, nor is it a walk in the park. We are dealing with destiny here. Not only yours, but your children and your children's children destinies are affected. In this hour, we must get adamant about finding within ourselves the kind of pit-bull tenacity that God's holy Apostles and Prophets had in the days they walked here on Earth. There is a remnant, a seed, and a residue left here, where not only the Prophets and Apostles walked, but where Jesus Himself walked here on Earth. These are the things that need to be resurrected in this hour. These are the gifts, the anointings, and the grace that need to be brought back full circle so we can reach a lost and dying world for our Lord and Saviour, Jesus Christ. Soldiers of God, we are agents of change. We are God's undercover agents with governmental power, sent into this Earth to bring about a change that will be eternal for the sake of God and His kingdom. When Jesus was sent to the Earth, the scripture declares that His government was upon His shoulders. (See Isaiah 9:6). *"For unto us a child is born, unto us a son is given: and the government shall be upon his shoulder: and his name shall be called Wonderful, Counsellor, The mighty God, The everlasting Father, The Prince of Peace."* The word "government" used here is the Hebrew word "mishrah," which translates: empire or government. I would also like to include the words: authority, rank, reign, glory, and power. Because God is in us, His glory, power, reign, government, authority, peace, healing, and deliverance is in us as well. Do you see now what it means to be a king's child, and the blessings we can receive as we submit to Christ's reign and authority in our lives? The other word found in Hebrew for "government," in reference to Isaiah 22:21, is the word "memshalah," which translates: rule, a ruler, dominion, government, power to rule. So, again, we see that God has all power to rule and reign here and in the heavenlies, but He had His Son, Jesus Christ, die that we might have dominion here in the Earth and invade and occupy the places that Satan has taken over. It states in Isaiah 19:17 that Judah shall be a terror unto Egypt, so shall we be anointed to become a terror unto our enemies. In Jesus Name!

We are so full of Holy Ghost power; that is, if you have been saved and asked specifically for the baptism of the Holy Ghost according to Luke 3:16. This scripture talks about us being baptized with Holy Ghost and fire, as well as being baptized in water as the outward symbol of our salvation in Jesus Christ.

Do we have the faith to ask God to take us deeper in Him, so we can tap into some deeper spiritual truths that lie in the heart and mind of Christ; truths that are found in the ancient texts of the Bible?

Chapter 3: Pit-Bull Tenacity

Looking through the pages of the Book of Life, we find that there were a certain group of believers in the early church. These believers were converted over to Christianity from all kinds of pagan belief systems, including some from backgrounds of witchcraft and idolatry. As stated before, Jesus Christ was a planet-shaker, and so was this bunch. These leaders were known as Christ's "sent ones" or God's holy Apostles.

(Ephesians 2:18-22): *"For through Him, we both have access by one spirit unto the Father. Now therefore ye are no more strangers and foreigners, but fellow citizens with the saints, and of the household of God: And are built upon the foundation of the apostles and prophets, Jesus Christ Himself being the chief cornerstone; In whom all the building fitly framed together groweth unto an holy temple in the Lord: In whom ye also are builded together for an habitation of God through the spirit."*

We too take part in this heavenly calling, as did the Apostles who were trained by Jesus Christ Himself. This is in reference to John 14:12 which tells us that greater things we shall do because He (Jesus) went unto the Father. We have been anointed and appointed just as the Apostle Paul, and the same power that lies in Jesus lies in you; the same spirit that parted the waters and calmed the winds and the waves lives and dwells in you. Adding to that, the scriptures declare that the same spirit that raised up Jesus Christ from the dead, lives and dwells in you. (See Romans 8:11).

Earlier, we discovered how Jesus came and brought a radical shift to the dynamics of how ministry had taken place, and now we see there is a radical group of believers and leaders who are willing to risk all for the sake of God's kingdom. Challenge yourself to take the time as you read this book to give your life a quick overview, and see if you should not step things up a little more than what you are currently operating in. We all are capable of more. We all are called to be more than conquerors here in the Earth. The Bible declares that the meek shall inherit the Earth. We certainly are not going to inherit the Earth when we are in Heaven. Why would we want Earth when we will have and behold all the beauties of Heaven? What more will we have to gain? We are here on Earth now, so it is time to get busy. We all have work to do. It is time to take dominion and authority over this Earth, and all that is in it! It is time to come forth with boldness and declare with our mouths what rightfully belongs to us as heirs of the kingdom of Heaven. It is time, and the season is now. Get to digging! Dig deep and don't you dare stop until that well flows with the overflowing water of the rivers of life that are in Christ Jesus. I want to provoke you to pursue your destiny, your hope, and your future that you have in Christ Jesus. I want to cheer you on as you cross over to the victory side and live that abundant life that Jesus Christ promises we shall and can all have here on the Earth. Even Deuteronomy 8:18 proclaims: *"But thou shalt remember the Lord thy God; for it is He that giveth thee power to get wealth, that He may establish His covenant which He sware unto thy fathers, as it is this day."*

That is the kind of dominion I am talking about; we shall and can have, right now, in Jesus Name!

3 John 2 reads: *"Beloved, I wish above all things that thou mayest prosper and be in health, even as thy soul prospereth."*

Psalm 1:1-3 reads: *"Blessed is the man that walketh not in the counsel of the ungodly, nor sitteth in the seat of the scornful. But his delight is in the law of the Lord: and in His law doth he meditate day and night. And he shall be like a tree planted by the rivers of water, that bringeth forth his fruit in his season; his leaf also shall not wither; and whatsoever he doeth shall prosper."*

These are dominion verses, and they are guaranteed to work for us every time. The Holy Ghost once told me that if I would work the Word, then the Word would work for me! Yes, that is why it says in the book of James that we are to be doers of His

Word and not hearers only, deceiving your own selves. (See James 1:22). (Read also verses 23-25).

Having pit-bull tenacity and an aggressive Godly spirit is key for obtaining victory and gaining ground because we are the children of God; therefore, we don't quit until that thing we are fighting for has been established. We must, then again, learn to decree and declare a thing forth with our mouth.

As we see in the book of Acts, the Apostles were so adamant and surefire about the call and destinies God had given them that they allowed for nothing to stand in their way. From beatings to persecution, in turmoil, strife, and imprisonments; they never gave up! They were dedicated and devoted to the promise the Father had given them. They were like Jesus: steadfast, unshakable, irrevocable, obstinate, bold, and broad-shouldered. They refused to be refused, and denied to be denied. They were planet-shakers; they were history makers and frontiersmen that blazed trails for you and me in ministry today. The Apostles stood up before governors and council men, and they received stripes and beatings. They were forbidden by city officials to preach the gospel of Jesus Christ in their regions, yet they refused. In fact, scripture portrays that in more than one instance, the Apostles were beaten, jailed, and forbade to preach; yet they went right back out just to do it all over again. Some people would say they were crazy, but they weren't crazy; they just had a zeal and a passion for the One who bled and died for them that they would be free! They knew that someday they would be able to see the eternal reward in Heaven that would await them for their eternal obedience unto God and Jesus Christ. These Apostles were so on fire for God that they laid hands on the sick and miracles happened before their very eyes.

These Apostles received the promise, and they held on to it in their hearts; this is very different from the culture we live in today. Today, if we do not get what we want, we cry and mope; we sit in doom and gloom pouting until finally someone gives us what we want. Well, those days are over. The fight is on. The battle of two kingdoms has begun, and the devil has waged war against the kingdom of God. Will we sit passively by and allow the devil to ruin our rewards, take our spoils, and plunder our seed? Will we stand by and watch the enemy abort our unborn children, and ruin the minds of the ones we already have now? Will we continue to allow our government to take prayer and God out of schools, all the while Eastern religions; including those with mysticism, witchcraft, and sorcery are taught to our children? Let's wake up, America. It is time to come home. Let's bring it back home. Let us awake and arise to the moral standard that God has stated for us in His Word that we should live by. The time is not near; the time is now. This is the clarion call not just to America, but to the nations. Let's move forward in progression and march to the cadence of the heartbeat of our Almighty God in Heaven. Will you march for Him? Let us go forward, for we are entering the battlefield.

CHAPTER 4: THE BATTLEFIELD

There are two kinds of wells that need to be re-dug. One is water wells. Water wells are wells that represent living water; the work of the wisdom of God within us. The other is oil wells. Oil wells are wells that are in us that have the anointing of the Holy Ghost all over it. As we see in the scriptures, oil is referred to as Holy Spirit often in the New Testament. We need to not only re-dig, but purge the existing wells and start digging new ones. But what do we do while there is a battle raging around us?

Let's go to the book of Nehemiah. Nehemiah is an Old Testament structure or example of the apostolic. Nehemiah was called to rebuild the walls of the city, but they could not do it without their weapons at hand. Thus is the same for you and me. The Apostle Paul declared unto us: *"For we wrestle not against flesh and blood, but against principalities, against powers, against the rulers of the darkness of this world, against spiritual wickedness in high places"* (Ephesians 6:12). Paul also declares in 2 Corinthians 10:4-6: *"For the weapons of our warfare are not carnal, but mighty through God, to the pulling down of strongholds; casting down imaginations, and every high thing that exalteth itself against the knowledge of God, and bringing into captivity every thought to the obedience of Christ; and having in a readiness to revenge all disobedience, when your obedience is fulfilled."*

These two verses of scripture alone prophecy that believers will be in a conflict. It will be, and already is a conflict between good and evil, light and darkness. Which kingdom are ye, I hear the spirit of the Lord asking. Because many will call on me in that hour, and I will have to reject them saith the Lord. Matthew 7:22-23 declares: *"Many will say unto me in that day, Lord, Lord, have we not prophesied in thy name? And in thy name have cast out devils? And in thy name done many wonderful works? And then will I profess unto them, I never knew you: depart from me, ye that work iniquity."*

Friends, we are in a war; the Earth prophecies it. We are in a war with a country that refuses and despises God, and it is a war that will not end because both sides are determined that their way is the right way. Well, there is only one way that is the right way, and that is the road that leads to Jesus. And I am sorry to say unto you new agers; there is not more than one way or path to get to God. The Bible clearly states: *"That if thou shalt confess with thy mouth the Lord Jesus, and shall believe in thy heart that God hath raised Jesus Christ up from the dead, thou shalt be saved. For with the heart man believeth unto righteousness; and with the mouth*

confession is made unto salvation" (Romans 10:9-10).
"Enter ye in at the strait gate: for wide is the gate, and broad is the way, that leadeth to destruction, and many there be which go in thereat: Because strait is the gate, and narrow is the way, which leadeth unto life, and few there be that find it" (Matthew 7:13-14).

There is only one way. There is one way up and one way down, and both paths lead to a place of which there is no return.

Are you willing to take the steps to live a life that is Holy, sold out, and on fire for Jesus Christ no matter what the cost? I urge you to seek God. He will never leave you nor forsake you. (See Hebrews 13:5). Also, He is a friend that sticketh closer than a brother. (See Proverbs 18:24).
Matthew 6:33: *"Seek ye first the kingdom of God and His righteousness: and all these things shall be added unto you."*
In this hour, we must learn to prioritize again and be able to put first things first.

It is worth the wait, and it is worth the fight. *"For since the beginning of the world men have not heard, nor perceived by the ear, neither have the eye seen, O God, beside thee, what he hath prepared for him that waiteth for him"* (Isaiah 64:4). Are you ready for what's to come?

CHAPTER 5: PURGING

No matter what walls need to be rebuilt, or whatever wells need to be re-dug, there has to first be a purging before it can be a success. In Nehemiah's day, had the land not been purged, or if there was not going to be a purging, there would be no sense of rebuilding in a place where no change is abound. The same is true inside of us! Before we can tap into new wells, (gifts that God has placed in our spirits) we must first be found faithful with what He has already given unto us. To whom much is given, much is required. (See Luke 12:48). The Bible also says to work out our own salvation with fear and trembling. (See Philippians 2:12).

Deep within man's spirit, there are wells that have not yet been tapped into. These places are portions of man's heart and spirit where God has imparted gifts, grace, and anointing. He imparted this while we were being knitted together in our mother's womb. Many of us despise heartache and trials, but it is in the time of the trying of our faith when greatness is birthed and pulled out of us. Many of our nation's leaders, and especially leaders in the kingdom of God, are those that have seen or been through some type of adversity. This adversity compelled them to press forward and push themselves greater into pursuing destiny. Generals in an army or branch of military did not become Generals because they were handed the stars or ranks on their jacket. Instead, they proved themselves while being tested and tried. Through the storm, through the rain, on the battlefield, and off the battlefield, they have received their ranks. So it is in the kingdom of Heaven. God always exalts or promotes the man, whom humbles himself. Look at the account of Jesus being led by the spirit of God into the wilderness to be tempted of the devil. (See Luke 4). Here, you will find that Jesus was led through a series of temptations and trials, each of which He would not succumb, nor would Jesus bow down. Finally, Jesus spoke up and declared: *"It is written, That man shall not live by bread alone, but by every word of God"* (Luke 4:4).

We too, must get this kind of boldness, and learn to stand up against the devil in the hour of temptation and in the times of adversity. If we are ever going to make it in this hour, we must be ones that know and believe that God is not just a God of peace, but He is a God of war, and He wars against the kingdom of darkness.

The Bible says in 1 John 3:8 *"For this purpose, the Son of God was manifested, that He might destroy the works of the devil..."* We can and will overcome every trial, obstacle, and temptation because the

Word of God declares: *"Ye are of God little children, and have overcome them: because greater is he that is in you, than he that is in the world"* (1 John 4:4). We are truly more than conquerors as the Word declares that we are what God's Word says we are, and whatever God's Word says we can do we can do it! Psalm 34:19-20 reads: *"Many are the afflictions of the righteous, but the Lord delivereth him out of them all. He keepeth all his bones: not one of them is broken."*

Psalm 119:71: *"It is good for me that I have been afflicted; that I may learn thy statutes."* Afflictions come, but afflictions go. The point is: we are not to make friends with our afflictions and develop soul ties with them. We are simply supposed to chalk them up to experience, glean the wisdom and knowledge from them, and pick up and move on because this is what a true soldier does. A true soldier does not lie down on the battlefield because he got wounded. Instead, he picks up his weapons, and he carries on with the assignment or the mission. This is true kingdom spirit and assignment as well. Look at David. The one whom the Bible says was a man after God's own heart. Do you think David was labeled that for his adultery or his failures? No. Do you think that David was labeled a man after God's own heart for making peace? David did not make peace; He declared war, and he fought until the finish, and until all his enemies were conquered. David was a warrior at heart and a king in spirit, and David was bold. These are the three qualities that made David a man after God's own heart. Look at the Apostles in the New Testament, especially in the book of Acts. They obtained boldness, and they did not back down for anyone or anything.

The same is true for us. If we refuse to back down, there will come a point in time when God will take over for us. Then the battle will shift from an attack against us, to becoming the Lord's battle simply because we are God's children. Anyone who opposes us or contends with us will have to contend with our God. (See 2 Chronicles 20:15, Isaiah 49:25, and Isaiah 41:11).

Know this: the true character of a man is honed out on the battlefield. Whatever battle you are facing; you were born for the battle, and fit for the fight. God has already anointed you to conquer. Isaiah 65:24 states, *"And it shall come to pass, that before they call, I will answer; and while they are yet speaking, I will hear."* Before you cried out to God, and before your storm or trial came, God already saw the battle, and He already developed in you the spirit to overcome it in Jesus Name.

If you have been through a trial, no matter how severe, God can deliver you and translate you in an instant into the place of destiny that He has orchestrated for you to be, in Him in this season. We must be like David, who said: *"For by thee I have run through a troop: by my God have I leaped over a wall"* (2 Samuel 22:30 and Psalm 18:29).

When it comes to battles and trials, fear not what man can do to you; neither be dismayed for the Lord our God whom is in Heaven will fight for us if we trust in Him and give it all up to Him.

God told Jeremiah to fear not their faces. In addition, Paul told Timothy, *"For the Lord has not given us the spirit, of fear, but of power, and of love and of a sound mind."* (2 Timothy 1:7) (See also Jeremiah 1:8, Jeremiah 1:17, and Ezekiel 2).

So, I encourage you to press forward in that battle you are fighting and face it. Face it and stand up to it, and do not back down until it has been conquered. Being conquered is not an option as we are God's children, and we are ambassadors for Christ Jesus delegated to be His mantle carriers in this earth, in this season in time.

Chapter 6: Walking in the Promise

If we choose to conquer, stay, and fight, we are assured the victory. We as children of the Most High God in Heaven, are fighting from the victory side as Jesus Christ has already conquered the cross: This includes death, hell, and the grave. (Philippians 2:8) records: *"And being found in fashion as a man, he humbled himself, and became obedient unto death, even the death of the cross."* (Galatians 3:13): *"Christ hath redeemed us from the curse of the law, being made a curse for us: for it is written, Cursed is every man that hangeth on a tree."*

We are heirs of Jesus Christ, and even though we may have afflictions, we carry in us the promise of eternal life, as well as our blessings here on Earth. (See Psalm 1 and Deuteronomy 28:1-14).

The promise is given unto them who will choose to conquer, and for those that trust in God by faith knowing that *"faithful is He that calleth you, who also will do it.* (1 Thessalonians 5:24). No matter what, God is on your side. *"Call unto me and I will answer thee, and show you great and mighty things which thou knowest not"* (Jeremiah 33:3).

We do not have to lack for wisdom when it comes to knowing the will, call, and the plans of God. God promises to speak to us, and declare His mighty works unto us; God promises to be our comforter, counselor, and guide. We must trust in Him fully knowing that He is God, and we are not. "Let go and let God," as the saying goes. I believe a lot of times we fight too hard, and we wear ourselves out. This is actually a ploy of the enemy, and a plot that Satan uses to distract us from entering into the promises of God.

You see; the promise of God always lies ahead, but many road blocks have been set in your path. These road blocks can be the enemy using family, friends, peers in ministry, or peers at work to come against you and hinder the work of God in your life. I have come to the understanding that most people do not even know they are being used by Satan to distract or hinder you from pursuing and reaching God's destiny. Most folks are ignorant to the devices of Satan as Paul mentions in Ephesians 6. (See also 2 Corinthians 1:8, Romans 1:13, and 1 Thessalonians 2:18).

I hear the Holy Ghost speaking in my spirit, no more hindrance in this hour. The God of Heaven, and the God of Abraham, Isaac, and Jacob, shall see to it that you get to the places that He has destined you to be in this hour. God shall see to it that your enemies are bound. They that are of you shall rejoice with you, and they that are not of you shall laugh and jeer at you not knowing that their day is coming.

God is saying that in this hour and season, He is about to halt your enemies right in their tracks. Just like in the days of the great deliverance of His people out of the hand of Pharaoh, God is about to cause the flood waters to overflow and overtake your enemies and the pharaohs who are invading your life. The only invasion that is about to come next is the Holy Spirit invading the lives of His people, overtaking them, and putting in them and on them His glory, power, and anointing to get the job done. The Holy Ghost is empowering His people right now, the very second as we speak. God is not a man that He should lie. (See Numbers 23:19).

We as the children of the God in Heaven shall walk in and take hold of the promises of God for the promises of God are yes and amen. (See 2 Corinthians 1:20).

What are the promises of God, you might ask?

Whatever God's Word says you can have, you can have. Everything in it from cover to cover. God is all about blessing His children and seeing to it that they walk in destiny, and that He is provider, Jehovah Jireh for them in every area and aspect of their lives. Hallelujah; we serve a God whose resources never run out, nor do they ever run dry. God is the well and the reservoir from which fresh and new living water flows freely to us each and every time we call on Him! God is concerned with blessing you and prospering you. 3 John 2 says: *"Beloved, I wish above all things that thou mayest prosper and be in health, even as thy soul prospereth."* God is enthused with blessing His people, but only if we get enthused about the things of the kingdom and the things that concern Him. James 1:27 declares: *"Pure religion and undefiled before God, and the Father is this, to visit the fatherless and the widows in their affliction, and to keep himself unspotted from the world."* If we do this, God will do that! He will bless us, keep us, prosper us, increase us, heal us, and deliver us every time we are in a time of need in Jesus Name! We are to be doers of the Word and not hearers only. (See James 1:22).

God's favor is included in His promises. As we obey God, God will release unto us His blessed peace and promises, as He did for Abraham when Abraham sojourned into an unknown land chasing after the promises of God. (Read Hebrews 11). Just as the forefathers pursued after God; God pursued and chased them down with wealth, riches, blessings, children, family, fields, lands, and so on. God is adamant about pursuing His children, hunting them down, and giving good gifts unto them. *"Every good gift and every perfect gift is from above, and cometh down from the Father of lights, with whom is no variableness, neither shadow of turning"* (James 1:17).

Why would God pursue you in order to bless you? Deuteronomy 8:18 reads: *"But thou shalt remember the Lord thy God: for it is He that giveth thee power to get wealth, that He may establish His covenant which he sware unto thy fathers as it is this day."* The word "wealth" here is the Hebrew word "chayil," which translates: a force; whether of men, means, or other resources. An army, wealth, virtue, valor, strength, able, activity, army, band of men or soldiers, company, great forces, goods, host, mighty power, riches, strength, strong, substance, train, valiant, valour, war, worthy, worthily.
This verse of scripture carries a wealth of information and elements that can be obtained through serving God and obeying Him.

I pray that you are ready to obey Him, trust by faith, and cross over into the promise that God has destined for you in this hour and season. Are you ready for what's to come?

Chapter 7: Pursuing

The Bible says that the kingdom of God suffereth violence and the violent take it by force. If we are ever going to obtain the things that God has in store for us, we not only need pit bull-tenacity, but we are going to have to study our enemy out as he does us. We are going to have to conquer and overcome with even more aggression than David or even Jehu did.

I love the story of Jehu and his characteristics, as I consider him an apostle of war. Jehu was the king whom God had Elijah anoint and appoint, and the king who ended up destroying the household of Ahab and that wicked queen Jezebel. Jezebel was such a wicked queen that she had murdered an innocent man of God that had a vineyard, and that man's name was Naboth. Naboth had a vineyard, and Ahab (Jezebel's husband) desired and lusted after it. We must look at this story intently and discern it with spiritual eyes of understanding and discernment.

A vineyard represents fruit, or what I refer to as our fruit, or our anointing. Ahab did not necessarily want the man of God's land as much as he lusted and pursued after destroying the man of God's character, fruit, and anointing. He whined like a little baby and refused to eat until Jezebel had Naboth murdered. What a weak-kneed, no back-bone, little wuss bag. Sounds like many so-called Christians today.

God's Word says to touch not God's anointed, nor do His prophets no harm. (Read 1 Chronicles 16:22 and Psalm 105:15).

Serve the devil notice before continuing. Tell him that he will not go any further in his attack to pursue you, God's child, in these final days and hours. Satan's days are numbered and surely he knows it, and it is okay to let him be aware of it as well.

If you read the account of Jehu in the book of 1 Kings, you will find that Jehu rode his chariot furiously into town and destroyed all that were of King Ahab and Jezebel's family and lineage. Like a mad man is how Jehu rode his chariot. (Also Read 2 Kings 9:20).

The Bible does say, "blessed are the peacemakers," but sometimes you have to fight for freedoms in order to obtain peace. I am not talking about physical violence here; the point is just as the Bible says, *"For the weapons of our warfare are not carnal, but mighty through God, to the pulling down of strongholds"* (2 Corinthians 10:4). A spiritual warfare is taking place now in the spirit realm as we speak. We must be discerning in this hour.

If one wants to pick a fight, there is no need to because the devil is already looking for you. The Bible says Jesus told Peter that Satan had desired to have him that he may sift him as wheat. (See Luke 22:31). Also, Satan came to God and God permitted Satan to attack Job. (See Job 1:1-8). The Bible also declares that Satan is the prince of the power of the air according to Ephesians 2:2. 1 Peter 5:8 also tells us that Satan is a roaring lion seeking whom he may devour. There are plenty of verses, including many more not listed here, that reveal to us the believer that Satan is a terrorist, and the only way to defeat a terrorist is not by avoiding him, but by conquering and overcoming him. Through the blood of Jesus and the mind of Christ, we can outwit every demon and every devil released at us at any given time and season. No matter where we are, God is on our side and always will be as long as we live to serve and obey Him.

If we are ever going to pursue the promise and obtain it, we are going to have to ask the Holy Spirit to baptize us with a spirit of Holy Ghost boldness that is much like what Stephen had in the book of Acts. The scripture records in Acts 6 that there was a man named Stephen whom was full of the Holy Ghost and with wisdom. As they stoned him, he still cried out to God to forgive his persecutors, much like Jesus did when He was giving up the ghost after suffering the cruel death on the cross.

We too must be this bold in this hour. After all, we are Nazarites, and Nazarites do not quit; we do not back up, back down, nor do we cower. Blessed be the name of the Lord.

So, I encourage you. Pursue!!!

Chapter 8: The Past is Over

Paul admonished us in Philippians 3:13-14:
"Brethren I count not myself to have apprehended: but this one thing I do, forgetting those things which are behind, and reaching forth unto those things which are before, I press toward the mark for the prize of the high calling of God in Christ Jesus".

If we are ever going to pursue, overtake, and stake claim on our promised land; if we are ever going to take hold of our rightful places and possessions, we are going to have to forget about the past. This includes our last battles and struggles.

Never forget about the victory God in Christ Jesus has brought us through, but we are to forget the troubles that came with it, as it will serve as a major distraction in the present and future of what God has in store for us.

We must learn that there are elements to the process of re-digging wells. The process brings forth progress, and progress gives birth to the promise. God has orchestrated every aspect and element of the story, and your story will become your testimony. Your testimony will eventually serve as the anointed element that will in turn lead to the deliverance of someone else. Stand strong, don't run, but allow every element in its season to run its course as you will be making progress, even though you may feel like you are not. Remember His strength is made perfect in weakness. (See 2 Corinthians 12:9).

Forgetting what lies behind clears our minds, cleanses our conscience, and allows for fresh revelation to be poured in by God. This revelation is sent to equip us with the mentality, wisdom, knowledge, and discernment needed to fight the fight in this hour in order to pursue.

Re-digging the wells of our spiritual forefathers is re-digging the faith that the patriarchs of the Bible, and even past generations once operated in. Now, I know we do not want to be clones of anyone, but what we do need in this hour is a renewed faith in Christ Jesus, as His Word says that He has given unto every man a measure of faith. (See Romans 12:3).

The word "measure" used here derives from the Greek word "metron." Metron means a measure, a limited portion, and/or a degree.

God has given unto every man a portion of faith to a certain degree, but please know that degree has much to do with temperature, and just as a temperature can be raised, so it is with our faith. Faith has no limits. That is why the word of God says in Isaiah 40:31 that we shall mount up with wings as eagles and soar. Eagles have no heights; they just ascend to their maximum altitudes and soar, and so it is with our faith. Once God gives us a measure of faith, it is His intent that that faith be built upon, expanded upon, and increased. How can faith be increased? Romans 10:17 reads : *"So then, faith cometh by hearing, and hearing by the Word of God."* If God has truly dealt to every man a measure of faith, then why are we not seeing miracles in our midst? The answer is easy, and is summed up into one word: fear. If we are not operating in faith, then we have chosen the element of fear to overtake our lives. Fear is the opposite of faith and they repel one other. The strength of our faith or our fear is determined by how much power and determination we give to it. We can delegate and grant jurisdiction to one or the other, and most of the time, it is a result of man's own will. Self-confidence has a lot to do with operating in the faith and choosing to use faith rather than allowing fear to enter in. When we choose faith, we then invite God to come be in our midst because faith is what pleases God. I believe it is the only act that pleases God as a matter of fact. (See Hebrews 11:1 and Hebrews 11:6).

Hebrews 11:6 declares that without faith, it is impossible to please God.

Mark 11:22-24: *"And Jesus answering saith unto them, have faith in God. For verily I say unto you, that whosoever shall say unto this mountain, be thou removed, and be thou cast into the sea; and shall not doubt in his heart, but shall believe that those things which he saith shall come to pass; he shall have whatsoever he saith. Therefore I say unto you, what things so ever ye desire, when ye pray, believe that ye receive them, and ye shall have them."*

Luke 17:5-6: *"And the apostles said unto the Lord, Increase our faith. And the Lord said, If ye had faith as a grain of mustard seed, ye might say unto this sycamine tree, Be thou plucked up by the root, and be thou planted in the sea; and it shall obey you."*

Faith is an important ingredient to utilizing the power of God at work in our lives, along with utilizing His glory, anointing, power, and favor. Faith is what translates us from the Earth realm to the spiritual realm and finally into the kingdom of Heaven where Jesus Christ, dwells. According to Romans 8, we are to walk in the spirit and not obey the lusts of the flesh. Spirit is a realm. We must learn to become a people that is comfortable only dwelling in the realm where Jesus Christ, Father God, and the Holy Spirit dwells. If we are not walking in the spirit and operating in it, then chances are we have become friends with the world and turned away from intimacy and true relationship with God. Friendship with the world makes us the enemy of God. James 4:4 states: *"Ye adulterers and adulteresses, know ye not that the friendship with the world is enmity with God? Whosoever therefore will be a friend of the world is the enemy of God."*

Faith is what picks us up, carries us into the realms of God's glory, and raises us up into His loving arms as we find ourselves in times of distress and calamity. God intervenes when he sees that faith is taking hold and taking charge in our lives, especially in our times of weakness.

This is why renewing our faith in God is so important and re-digging the wells of our spiritual forefathers is so important. If faith is not important, then why did scripture say that we are to believe in our hearts and confess with our mouths that we should be saved? (See Romans 10:9).

If faith was not important, then why did Jesus rebuke the disciples and say, "Oh ye of little faith" when they could not rebuke the wind and the waves or trust in God to do so?

If faith is not important, then why did God tell Jeremiah to fear not the faces of them as seen in Jeremiah 1:8?

Faith is the key that unlocks the blessings and miracles from the kingdom of Heaven into the sphere or realm of where we often dwell. Faith is the substance of things hoped for, the evidence of things unseen. (See Hebrews 11:1).

Faith is the activator of the miracles of God, the destructor of fear, and the element that unlocks and unleashes God's favor into our lives. Faith is knowing God....period.

We do not need more faith; we just need to spend more time in God's presence because He is faith. We need less of us and more of Him. We need to decrease so that He will increase. (See John 3:30).

Faith is knowing God and God dwelling in us.

To know God is to stare eternity, peace, hope, and healing in the face; it helps us to know and have an assurance that God is for us and not against us. That is true assurance; that is blessed assurance, and there is no better insurance policy than that.

Chapter 9: Faith Established

Romans 10:17: *"So then faith cometh by hearing, and hearing by the Word of God."*

If we are never in a position to hear the Word of God, we will never be able to receive the miraculous impartation from the Word of God. According to John 1:1: *"In the beginning was the Word, and the Word was with God, and the Word was God."*
John 1:14: *"And the Word was made flesh and dwelt among us, (and we beheld His glory as of the only begotten of the father,) full of grace and truth."*

To be established in the faith is to be certain that the God we serve is as real as the words on these pages, or to be as close as the nose on our faces. God is real, and He is breathing fresh breath and life upon us, even right now. God's Word is God-breathed, and the very reason you are alive right now is because God has chosen to breathe His breath of Life upon you. The God of Heaven, the Creator of Heaven and earth has blessed us with this gift we call life.

How do we get the glory of God so strong on us like the other renowned men of faith? One must first set himself apart from man, the things of the world, and the influences of the world. He must sanctify, cleanse, and purify through fasting and prayer. Worship must be part of the believer's life, not just daily, but momentarily. In order to walk in the glory and the power of God, we must be in continual communication with God. We must remain in an attitude of obedience and worship toward God, not just because we want to or have to, but because we so desire. Worship and spending time in God's presence happens because we are so knitted, rooted, and grounded in Him.

Pertaining to marriage, the Bible says that the two become one flesh. The Bible also defines us, which are in the body, as the bride of Christ, with Him being the bridegroom. When we get saved, we become one with Him; therefore, just as a spouse is intimate with their partner, God desires intimacy with us because we too are wedded to Him. Intimacy is worship, honor, obedience, agreement with His Word, having faith, and honoring God in every aspect of our lives. All of these are key elements to the releasing of God's glory into our lives and seeing the manifest power and presence of God being bestowed upon us.

Webster's Online Dictionary defines the word "established" in this way: To make stable or firm.

To fix immovably or firmly. To appoint or constitute for permanence. To enact, or ordain. To originate and secure the permanent existence of. To found, to institute, to create, to regulate. To place advantageously in a fixed condition.

To be rooted and grounded is one thing, but to be established is another. This is where Jesus Christ so desires for us to be in this hour. Established and fixed in a state of permanence in Him, His kingdom, and His principles.

To be established in God is the surety that we will never leave Him as He promises in His Word that He will never leave us nor forsake us. (See 1 Kings 8:57 and Deuteronomy 31:8).

In this hour, we must believe God for everything, and nothing else should matter to us except pleasing Him. If we do not live to please God and seek Him first, we are just wearing ourselves out, beating around a bush, and spinning in circles because the greatness that lies within you will never be found without finding you in Christ Jesus. If you trust in man more than God, and you trust in your resources more than God, you already displayed a lack of faith, which is noted as sin. Without faith, it is impossible to please God. (See Hebrews 11:1). Remember, friendship with the world makes us the enemy of God.

To be established would also mean that we are trusting fully in God in every aspect and area of our lives, no matter what the outcome. Are you worried about money, family, relationships, finances? We spend more time trying to get the world to like us than we do in seeking God's favor and acceptance. If we would just invest the time into passionately pursuing God, God will give us all the favor, resources, and relationships we need to succeed in this hour.

If you have to be so busy trying to pursue man's acceptance and approval, that is a sure sign that you need a renewed faith in God.

On a personal note, one thing that really bothers me is how churches, ministries, and leaders get all bent out of shape when someone leaves their church as if the bills will no longer get paid. We must learn not to develop such soul ties with man, and just trust God. If someone wants to leave, God will replace him. If it was Satan that caused that person to go, do we not know that God will make the enemy give back seven times as much as what was stolen once that thief has been found out? This is scriptural. We need to get back to believing in God and not man. We need to learn to look at the things which are unseen and hidden in God through Christ Jesus. We need to trust that if God established the work, He will be faithful to carry it on to completion. (See Philippians 1:6).

If they want to go, let them go. Increase comes from God and not man! Personally, I have too much on my plate, and too big of a schedule to worry about wiping tears and wiping rears. It is time to grow up and mature in the Lord and graduate from the milk to the meat of God's Word. Even the apostles said that it was not right for them to neglect the ministry of the word of God in order to wait on tables. (See Acts 6:2). Faith is refusing to believe the report of what we see, think, feel, or hear. We are not called to believe man's report. It does not matter what man says, if God's Word didn't say it, then we are not called to believe it. That is showing true signs of being established in God; being rooted and grounded in the faith.

I encourage you to look to the Lord for all things for He is a friend that sticketh closer than a brother. God will be your counselor, way-maker, friend, lover, and brother. God will be your spouse, help-mate, finance director, and so on. God will see to it that your enemies are bound and that your body is healed. These are only a few benefits of being part of the kingdom of God, being rooted and grounded in Him, and being rooted in the faith that comes through Him.

Proverbs 3:5-6 reads: *"Trust in the Lord with all thine heart; and lean not unto thine own understanding, In all thine ways acknowledge Him, and He shall direct thy paths."*

If you will stay fixed and focused on God, the benefits and the blessings will begin to pour out on you, and you will never want to run back to the world or the enemy's camp.

Faith is going into the enemy's camp and taking back what he stole from you. This is the kind of anointing that this generation has been anointed and graced with.

Sometimes you have to tell the devil that enough is enough, and you are coming to get your stuff. Declare and serve notice on the devil that the repossession order has been made out in Heaven, and we are about to take the Earth and all its occupants back for the Lord God, the Creator of Heaven and of Earth.

The Bible declares that the Earth is the Lord's and the fullness thereof. It also says that He owns the cattle on a thousand hills, and that power belongs unto God. (See 1 Corinthians 10:26, Psalm 50:10, and Psalm 62:11). If God owns the world, and we are His children and heirs of Christ Jesus; that could only mean what belongs to the King belongs to the King's child.

In this hour, God is re-establishing the faith that once was back into the hearts of man and women alike, and at the same time, He is adding to it His own unique touch. Right now, God is maximizing and increasing the faith of His people to believe again in Him for signs, wonders, and miracles to follow.

Take hold of faith and let faith take hold of you; it is time to get your marching orders and move forward in the things of God. In this hour, God's true believers are going to obtain the things in the Earth that are needed to get the job done. Seeing that souls get saved and reaching a lost and dying world is the number-one goal on the heart of Jesus Christ.

Are we ready to align our hearts with God's plan and design? Are we ready to give up the things that bring us comfort in this hour so we can move in obedience to God by faith, like faithful Abraham did as he sojourned into an unknown land and amongst a strange nation? Abraham became the father of many nations by making sacrifices and obeying every word God gave him to obey.

Chapter 10: Revival for the Fittest

I have recently been studying many of the revivals of the past, and there is one in particular that truly impacted my heart. I am sure that the hearts of many others were impacted by it as well.

The Azusa Street revival began in 1906 and lasted until 1916. This revival was known for many different cultures coming together in unity. People witnessed God moving in signs, wonders, and miracles; including the evidence of speaking in tongues. It was also known that at or around that same time frame, there were other revivals breaking out. A couple of other well-known revivals included the Welsh revival, which was held in 1904 in Wales. There was a revival that broke out before both of these in Topeka, Kansas called the Topeka outbreak. While each revival was powerful, and there were many different experiences as the Holy Spirit released His glory, each individual revival had their strong points. Some revivals operated strongly in supernatural healings and miracles; some baptisms of the Holy Spirit with the evidence of speaking in other tongues, and some received ministry calls and went right out preaching the gospel and leading others to the Lord. Many churches were planted as a result of these revivals, and many missionaries went to the mission fields. We are about to experience the same outbreaks in our nation and around the world today! As I have been praying, I have been seeing open portals over certain cities and regions, and the Holy Spirit has been showing me like a whirling in the atmosphere above these cities and regions. I believe that the whirling of the clouds I see is spiritual and represents the kingdom of God manifesting, but the kingdom of darkness being swallowed up by the prayers and intercession of God's believers. In this hour, if revival is going to break forth, it is going to take a renewing of our faith and a belief, and a boldness that our spiritual forefathers in the past had.

Abraham, Joshua, Moses, Jeremiah, and other prophets were pioneers. A pioneer is one whom treads into unknown territories, stakes claim to these territories. He then settles in these territories and establishes life, family, business, and ministry there.

The free online dictionary by Farlex defines a pioneer as: one who ventures into unknown, or unclaimed territory to settle; one who opens up new areas of thought, research, or development; a soldier who performs construction or demolition work, in the field to facilitate troop movements.

In my previous book, 'From Discipleship to

Apostleship,' I talked about the role that an apostle takes on, and what is required of them. As stated in the book, an apostle could be noted as or known as a General in the kingdom, as well as in the realm of faith. This is scriptural and can be seen in action in various areas of the Bible and notated in scripture; nevertheless, an apostle is not only a General or a high-ranking kingdom ambassador, but an apostle is a pioneer. A true apostle is a statesman, as well. Farlex Online Dictionary defines a statesmen this way: "A man who is a leader in national and in international affairs." That is what an apostle is. The Word of God declares in Acts 1:8: *"But ye shall receive power, after that the Holy Ghost is come upon you; and ye shall be witnesses unto me both in Jerusalem, and in all Judea, and in Samaria, and unto the uttermost part of the Earth."* The uttermost parts of the Earth represent it as international ministry. In addition, Farlex defines a statesman as: "a man who is a political leader regarded as a disinterested promoter of the public good."

We can liken that to King David. David was a king and a ruler over the people. Lastly, Farlex Online Dictionary defines a statesman as: "A man that is a respected leader in a given field." Statesmen are known to mostly be in government, politics, and areas of diplomacy. The same is true in the kingdom of Heaven. Ephesians 4:11-12 states: *"And He gave some, apostles, prophets, evangelists, and some pastors and teachers; for the perfecting (maturing) of the saints, for the work of the ministry, for the edifying of the body of Christ."* God was the very first to come up with delegated positions of authority; man did not. Therefore, when God calls a man, He also equips and anoints that man or woman to fulfill the call of God on their life. God never gives us more than what we can handle.

Warfare comes in when distractions are sent by the people and the enemy (Satan). Most of the time these distractions come to leaders through people usually orchestrated by Satan. This is called spiritual warfare. Always be cautious when a national leader is exposed or falls to the condemnation of man because no one knows the pressure and the strain that is on that man by being in the public spotlight. There is an intense amount of pressure on one as they are released into the spotlight on national and international levels. Pressure comes, and it doesn't matter if you are a governmental official, a news reporter, an author, song writer, or minister of the Word of God. Leaders are all nationally and internationally exposed, and they carry a great weight and mantle on their shoulders. Praise God for the leaders in the kingdom of God. God promises us in His Word that His yoke is light, and His burden is easy! That is, if we take heed and submit to the Father of Glory in and through Christ Jesus.

Every time someone falls, it is usually by sexual immorality, promiscuity, theft, or deception. Why is that? The reason is Satan; the master of deception is at work continually messing with the hearts and minds of man, creating pressure and confusion, and ultimately trying to get that great man to fall. Delilah had caused Sampson to fall. Bathsheba was David's snare. These were both great statesmen who held governmental positions in the kingdom of God. Both were tempted with lust, perversion, and overtaken with a spirit of whoredom. You can go through the pages and books of the Bible and find where many great leaders that were called by God, fell prey to the wiles and the temptations of the enemy. You will always find that the enemy had been setting up the ploy for a while. The greater the call, the greater the temptation Satan tries to set up on our paths. Nevertheless, those of us that are in the Lord do not have to fear, nor do we have to be afraid. We just need to be alert, prepared, and prayed up before the attacks and ploys of Satan are sent our way. Do not pour your heart out to a stranger or even to one that assumes or likens himself to be your friend. This is the approach of the enemy to find out your strategy of success with the intentions to destroy you, destroy your kingdom, and cause it to fall. Never share anything that God shares with you in secret to anyone. Only share it with God and your spouse. Remember the Bible says that Satan is the prince of the power of the air. That means that he is in the atmosphere, and he (Satan) is like a roaring lion seeking whom he may devour. (See Ephesians 2:2 and 1 Peter 5:8). If you notice, a lion seeks after and prowls like a cat after his prey. A lion hides and lurks in hidden places. It is like picking up a venomous snake, and it bites you. You knew it was a snake when you picked it up. That is the same with a lion. A lion is not a pet. It is an animal that ferociously seeks after and devours its prey. Leaders, be cautious, be sober, and be vigilant. Know at all times who is in your spheres. You never can be too cautious.

1 Peter 5:8 declares: *"Be sober, be vigilant; because your adversary the devil, as a roaring lion, walketh about, seeking whom he may devour."* Notice it says to "be sober." The Webster's Revised Unabridged Dictionary defines sober as: "Temperate, habitually temperate, not intoxicated, not wild or insane, a visionary, serious and subdued in habit, appearance and demeanor. Of sober judgment, and a man that has his senses. Passionate."

This is a very thorough and concise description of what the word "sober" means and so shall we be as our senses and discernment are sharpened. We are sharpened as we spend time in God's presence, and as we allow the wisdom of God to overtake our lives. As we submit ourselves wholly and fully to God, God will then give unto us the mind of Christ and the God-given ability to think out, discern, and accomplish that which He has laid before us to conquer and accomplish.

The next word we will look at is "vigilant." The Merriam Webster's Online Dictionary defines "vigilant" as: "being alertly watchful, especially to avoid danger. Also the dictionary refers to it as "being attentive, awake, alert, and watchful."

Paul said to the Galatians in Galatians 3:1: *"O foolish Galatians, who hath bewitched you, that you should not obey the truth, before whose eyes Jesus Christ hath been evidently set forth, crucified among you?"*

Ephesians 5:11-17: *"And have no fellowship with unfruitful works of darkness, but rather reprove them. For it is a shame even to speak of those things which are done of them in secret. But all things that are reproved are made manifest by the light: for whatsoever doth make manifest is light. Wherefore he saith, Awake thou that sleepest, and arise from the dead, and Christ shall give thee light. See then that ye walk circumspectly, not as fools, but as wise, redeeming the time, because the days are evil."*

So you see, we cannot ever be too cautious, and we are warned constantly through the Word of God about being alert, being awake, being sober, and being vigilant. There is an enemy on the loose and to believe otherwise means you have already been bewitched and duped by Satan, the prince of the power of the air; that evil one that works in the hearts of the children of darkness. We are of the Light. Ephesians 5:8: *"For ye were sometimes darkness, but now are ye light in the Lord: walk as*

children of light."
We must be sober and vigilant in this hour if we are ever going to survive the upcoming events that are about to arise in this current state of immorality that we live in.

Many people have this misconception about how revival is going to come to America and other cultures in this hour.

Let me just make this clear right off the start: Where there is no repentance, there will be no refreshing. Disobedience repels the blessing of God and His favor. Obedience and repentance attracts the favor of God, His forgiveness, and His blessings. Where there is no vision, the people perish. (See Proverbs 29:18). Remember, the word sober dealt with vision.

If we do not focus on repentance from immorality and idolatry, then we may as well kiss revival good-bye. Many will call me a critic and say that I am negative, but I didn't coin it; God did. In God's Word, it declares: *"For the wages of sin is death; but the gift of God is eternal life through Jesus Christ our Lord"* (Romans 6:23). Only the strong, the pursuant, and the persevering will survive. Matthew 11:12 states: *"And from the days of John the Baptist until now the kingdom of heaven suffereth violence, and the violent take it by force."* The devil is the greatest terrorist who ever lived. So it will be that the aggressive, persevering, and the passionate will be the ones still found standing in the day of final victory. Aggression, as referenced here is not physical violence; aggression means to be radical prayers, radical worshipers, and refusing to be reduced to the world's level. We are not of Babylon; therefore, we are called to come out of Babylon. The same with Sodom and Gomorrah. Paul told Timothy to be a good soldier and to do a good warfare with the prophecies that went out before him. (See 2 Timothy 2:3 and 1 Timothy 1:18).

2Timothy 2:3: *"Thou therefore endure hardness as good soldier of Jesus Christ."*

1 Timothy 1:18: *"This charge I commit unto thee, son Timothy, according to the prophecies which went before on thee, that thou by them mightest war a good warfare."*

As one can clearly see, these verses are not for the weak kneed and spineless. These particular verses are militant and bold in nature. They admonished Timothy and us to be bold, aggressive, and militant as we war a good warfare and fight a good fight. Christianity is not a playground, and if you think it is, then you will quickly become the devil's playground. One must realize that if he becomes a Christian, he has enlisted in an army that is on the winning side, but as with any war, you will find that your freedom and liberation out of the kingdom of darkness into the kingdom of light will not come cheap. The devil never likes to let anyone go once he has had him in his clutches for so long. Adam and Eve never belonged to Satan. Yet Satan had plotted a ploy to get them to fall and enter into darkness. What makes you think you are free from the attacks of the enemy? Again, these are statements that will get us accused of being negative, but those that make those kinds of accusations are the ones that are already duped by the enemy. The veil has been pulled over their eyes, and their minds are being blocked by demons of mental strongholds and oppression.

So, what is it then? Why is it so important to re-dig the wells of our spiritual forefathers? Our past fathers in the faith knew morality, but now we see immorality. They knew what being sold out to Jesus Christ was all about. The past men and women of the faith knew that walking with God would be a journey, but they went anyway. These were men and women who would go into places unknown with no money, no resources, one coat, and the assignment God had given them. God's Spirit went before them, and they believed in the ministry of angels. Today we have GPS systems, cell phones, laptops, satellites, Internet, email, and many other gadgets to navigate us. All of these gadgets are an asset and added benefit as well, but I often wonder how distracted from God we are by having all these accommodations. I believe all of us can agree that many of these things we have incorporated in our everyday life can be distracting.

Yet we find it hard to break away and spend more time with God. The only way we will get God's Glory on us is if we put some of these things down and get alone with God again. Ask yourself this question: If our bodies are temples of the Holy Spirit, can the Holy Spirit mingle Himself with the things of the world? Let us look back at the structure of the church in the Book of Acts and revisit the great miracles, signs, and wonders that took place in the masses. Many souls were saved, and the people of those days were passionate, sold out, on fire, and Holy-Ghost filled believers in Jesus Christ.

I believe that these are the days of Elijah, and the dry bones are becoming as flesh. There is an army of believers, the remnant, that the book of Revelation talks about that are rising up and pursuing the greatness that we have in and through Christ Jesus. We are the generation that is rising up in power and authority, and we are declaring the Word of the Lord boldly; breaking through all of the corridors of darkness. We are anointed to bust through Satanic wiles and schemes, and we are appointed by God to break every yoke of bondage including religion, legalism, and the occult spirit that has overtaken many churches. We are Nazarites. We are God's initiators, not imitators. We care about people, and we love God with all our heart. There is a group of us left out there, and we shall arise because it is our time to shine. It is our time to come forth, declare, and decree the Word of the Lord one more time to this generation in which we live. God is anointing people in this hour to destroy, break, and obliterate the powers of darkness that are attacking and afflicting many through generational curses. God is cleansing bloodlines in genealogies, and we are about to see the salvation of complete families take place in this last great outpouring of God's Spirit. We will usher in God's power and presence, just as Paul said in 1 Corinthians 2:4-5: *"And my speech and my preaching was not with enticing words of man's wisdom, but in demonstration of the spirit and of power: That your faith should not stand in the wisdom of men, but in the power of God."* This sums it all up, and this is who we are.

Two words we need to look at here. The first one is demonstration. The word "demonstration" used here in this scripture text is the Greek word "apodeixis," which means: "manifestation. It can also refer to the Greek word "apodeiknumi," which means: to show off, exhibit, and demonstrate.

The word "power" is the Greek word "dunamis," which translates: "miraculous power, ability, abundance. Mighty worker of miracle, power, strength, violence, mighty (wonderful) work." (See 1 Corinthians 2:4-5). Again and we can safely say adding the Greek text to it, that the Holy Spirit was saying through the Apostle Paul that there was a mighty miracle working power on the inside of him. Paul was given the ability to demonstrate this power and cause it to manifest right in the people's very midst, and that same power and ability is alive and well on the inside of us right here, right now, even as we speak, I decree it and declare it in Jesus Name for you and me.

Mix repentance with the understanding and revelation of this word, and we will see revival break out right in our very midst.

Are you ready? Are you ready for what's to come?

Chapter 11: Signs and Wonders

1 Corinthians 2:4: *"And my speech and my preaching was not with enticing words of man's wisdom, but in demonstration of the Spirit and of power."*

Let us focus on the word "demonstration" once again. We know that it translates "manifestation" in the Greek text. The word "manifestation," according to the online dictionary by Farlex, translates as: "An indication of the existence, reality, or presence of something. One of the forms in which someone or something such as a person, a divine being, or an idea is revealed, and also, the materialized form of a spirit. A public demonstration usually of a political nature."
This is a great definition of "manifestation." As noted in my last book 'From Discipleship to Apostleship,' presence ministry is when the Holy Spirit so overtakes you that your very countenance is changed, and you are transformed. This is when everything you touch or even pass by gets blessed, healed, or delivered. As we get more submitted to God, God is dedicated to visiting His people and releasing His glory, power, and favor on their lives.

In Acts 5:15, we see the factual recorded story of Peter passing by certain people, and as he did so, many people were healed as he passed. Why do you think that is, and how could it be?

Two reasons: One reason is that Peter was so full of the Holy Ghost, just as you and I can be if we invite Him in our lives and mortal bodies. We must ask the Holy Spirit and permit Him to rule and reign in our lives. The second reason was Peter walked with God, and anytime one walks with God, His shadow will overshadow you so that the same saving, healing, and delivering anointing will be on you as well. I like to think of it as walking beside a big man; one that is taller than I. When the sun shines on him, it casts a shadow on me. This is the same in the spiritual. When God turns His face towards us, and shines His face upon us, the Light of the Father reflects down into the Earth realm, and the shadow of Jesus is cast upon us. And so shall it be in these last days as Satan is unleashing his last assault on the Earth as he knows his days are numbered. With all of the wars, rumors of war, earthquakes, and disasters in divers places; we are going to have to walk in an anointing that helps us overcome and be able to still function in our calling and elections. I was talking with someone the other day, and he made mention of how he could not imagine the heaps of dead bodies that lie in the streets after a tsunami or tidal wave strikes. Even tornadoes unleash a fury that creates gruesome results. Matthew 24 warns us of the impending danger and turmoil we will face in the last days.

Notice God does not warn us that it may happen, it says it shall happen. Matthew 24:7-8 reads: *"For nation shall rise against nation, and kingdom against kingdom, and there shall be famines and pestilences, and earthquakes in different places, and these are the beginning of sorrows."* It is going to require remaining in God's presence in order to be able to stand, let alone withstand what is about to come.

I am often reminded of the great Smith Wigglesworth. Wigglesworth was born in June of 1859, and lived until March of 1947. He came out of the Methodist church denomination, but later had an encounter with God, and he became known as a great Pentecostal evangelist. During Wigglesworth's years in ministry, many received miraculous healings, as the power of God was present in his meetings. At one point, the authorities in Sweden forbade Wigglesworth to lay hands on anyone, so he taught them to lay hands on themselves, and to believe God for their own healing. They did, and many were miraculously healed. It was also documented that throughout the course of Wigglesworth's ministry, the Holy Spirit of God had moved upon him and through him to raise several people from the dead, including his wife. Friends, this is not a myth. This is the power of God that is available to us as God declares to us in His Word that the same spirit that raised up Jesus Christ from the dead, lives and dwells on the inside of us. (See Romans 8:11).

It was also noted that Smith Wigglesworth preached at many Assemblies of God events, but never joined their denomination. Smith Wigglesworth also believed in the doctrine of laying of hands, and anointing with oil, as we see stated in James 5 in the Bible. He also prayed over prayer cloths, believing in the tangible transferable anointing of the Holy Spirit. We also see this is doctrinal in the book of Acts 19, as the Apostle Paul prayed over cloths, aprons, and handkerchiefs; and those that touched them were healed.

Biographies have revealed that God moved through Wigglesworth so powerfully up to twenty-three people were raised from the dead during his time in ministry. One account was of a woman who was brought into a meeting in a coffin, and she was raised up from the dead by the anointing and power of God. It was stated that the woman slapped Wigglesworth on the face and reprimanded him, telling him that she was in a far better place than here. Another account was a man in a funeral parlor already embalmed that was raised up from the dead. If you do not believe in the resurrection, how can you believe in God, seeing that He is the God of resurrection, and He raised Jesus Christ from the dead. How about the account of the prophet in the book of Ezekiel? God had taken him up in the spirit, and the Lord told him to prophesy unto the dead bones that the breath of God will come upon them once again, and sinews of flesh will come on their bones. Also it said in Ezekiel 37:12-14,

"Therefore prophesy and say unto them, Thus saith the Lord GOD; Behold, O my people, I will open your graves, and cause you to come out of your graves, and bring you into the land of Israel. And ye shall know that I am the LORD, when I have opened your graves, O my people, and brought you up out of your graves, And shall put my spirit in you, and ye shall live, and I shall place you in your own land: then shall ye know that I the LORD have spoken it, and performed it, saith the LORD." If this Biblical truth, along with Romans 8:11 does not convince us of the resurrection power of God, then it is definitely time for a renewed faith in God in America.

Smith Wigglesworth did not learn to read until after he got married, and it was his wife Polly that taught him how to read. I still today wonder if man is not getting too educated in the secular realm causing us to no longer believe God in the area of the miraculous and supernatural. Another interesting point is: Smith Wigglesworth would not permit a newspaper in his house. I do believe that today there is an ungodly influence that enters into our homes as we permit these things that are of the world to enter our home. My wife and I have come to the agreement that we will not watch news in our home, except on special occasions when there is a national event or something really important. Other than that, we believe that you can maintain such a close relationship with God, that if God wants you to know something, He is mighty enough to reveal it to us. News casts and reports release fear, anxiety, stress, turmoil, and strife into people's lives, homes, environments, and atmospheres.

I remember being in kindergarten when the first space shuttle exploded, and we were forced to watch it in school with the lights off. That memory is still depicted in my mind and it released fear into me. I was five-years-old and and this was traumatic for me. Images that showed the grief, turmoil, and strife that came on that unfortunate and somber day. The bottom line is we were too young to have been made to do such a thing. All the same, we are living in a day where the video games our children play are so gruesome and so graphic that it looks like real life as bloodshed is being depicted before their young, innocent eyes. What a shame, and what a long way from holiness our culture has become.

Many will say that you cannot keep your kids hidden and protected, but if you think that the public school system is going to help assist you in helping your kids grow in the wisdom and the knowledge of the Lord Jesus Christ, you need to look again. If you are only taking them to church for two hours on Sunday and that is all the God they are getting, the 30 hours of secular education they are getting is having a far deeper impact. What you spend most of your time doing, studying, or examining are the things that will be more deeply rooted in the caverns of your mind.

Bottom line: With everything, there is an influence. From television sitcoms, to soap operas, to Hollywood magazines, and news articles; all these things are releasing an image, and are embedding perceptions deep into the lives of our children, ourselves and the generations to come. If we do not get back to a place of purging through repentance, we will be a society that is as cold as the days of the Holocaust era. In fact, if you study that era, you will find that where we are today in our culture, and society is no different.

The whole point is if we are ever going to see society changed, and experience a demonstration of God's power and His love in our culture, we need to be detoxed of the impurities, cleansed from the idolatries, and purged of the wickedness that we have allowed to infiltrate our land. Saints, we let this happen. The church was designed by God to be an influence in regions, cultures, and politics just like it was in the days of the great apostles.

Like Wigglesworth, we must turn back to the things that are required of God for us to live lives that are holy and blameless. Holiness is possible. It is a matter of overcoming the will of our flesh. The book of James even teaches us that no man is tempted by God, but rather a man is tempted when he is drawn away and enticed by his own lust and enticed. (See James 1:12-16).

This is the appointed time of us seeking the will of

God, getting into His presence, and not leaving until we come back down from the mountain fully immersed by the power and glory of God. It was for this reason that God chose to put His Spirit on man so that God's glory could be revealed to man with the intention to draw men unto Him. The one and only true God, the author and finisher of our faith. In this hour, God is wanting to use us as His vessels as well, to be demonstrators of His glory, so that His manifest power and presence can be revealed to this world one last time before the return of the Lord of Glory, Jesus Christ. Yes, the return of Christ Jesus is nigh; it is very nigh. Are you ready? Are you ready for what's to come?

Chapter 12: It Is Our Time To Shine

Acts 28:8: *"And it came to pass, that the father of Publius lay sick of a fever and of a bloody flux: to whom Paul entered in, and prayed, and laid his hands on him, and healed him."*

Let us get one thing clear about the apostolic. True apostolic is moving and operating in God's anointing, glory, power, and governing authority at all times. It is just a part of who we are. It is as if God was a tree, and His roots were to get entwined into the depths of our hearts, souls, and spirits. Our minds are so full of desire to passionately pursue after our Master, our Lord and Savior Jesus Christ, who is the Chief Apostle. It is built in our ticker to tick the devil off, just as scripture says: *"He that committeth sin is of the devil; for the devil sinneth from the beginning. For this purpose the Son of God was manifested, that He might destroy the works of the devil"* (1 John 3:8). If Jesus came to destroy the works of the devil, and He lives in us; then what burns in God should be what burns in us also. That is if one desires to become like He is and be molded in His image.

True apostolic is being so full of the Holy Ghost

that everything we touch gets saved, healed, and delivered. True apostolic will expose darkness in every sphere, and it will also cause the devils to scream out in fear. True apostolic is not expecting man to provide for you, but rather utilizing whatever resources you have in hand at the current and present time, and watching God increase and multiply them.

Although these are just a few examples, I would not be doing anyone justice by not mentioning to you that operating in God's true apostolic authority will also attract many enemies and persecutors to you. Many will be envious of the level of glory and power that you operate in. This is a sad thing, but true. Although God's glory, power, love, and blessings is available to all; many do not want to pay the price for it, so they choose the lazy way out. The lazy way consists of murmuring about you, trying to destroy your character and ministry, with the hopes of being able to hijack it. What a deception the enemy places in the minds of man of today. What is truly happening is one is being set up by Satan for destruction, and ultimately death. The Bible declares that we are not to touch God's anointed, nor do His prophets any harm. (See 1 Chronicles 16:22 and Psalm 105:15). Be very careful that Satan is not using you to come against God's anointed, in any way, shape, or form. It is a set up from the enemy to get you into error so that the judgment of God will have to fall upon you. Let's revisit Acts 28:8: *"And it came to pass, that*

the father of Publius lay sick of a fever and of a bloody flux: to whom Paul entered in, and prayed, and laid his hands on him, and healed him."
If you notice, the scripture states this time that Paul had laid his hands on the father of Publius and Paul healed him. This verse reads the same in every translation, except for one translation; which states Paul had made him well, rather than healed Him. It still is the same concept.

Did you know that when you get saved, you now take on the DNA of Jesus Christ? You are of a new bloodline. You have been adopted and grafted into a kingdom that carries an anointing to destroy yokes, lift burdens, break chains, heal the brokenhearted, save souls, and deliver the demon-possessed. As we get sold out for Jesus He puts His Spirit on us and in us, and we now become super-naturalists because the supernatural One lives and dwells on the inside of us. We have been given the ability and the authority to lay hands on the sick, and cast out demons in Jesus Name. (See Mark 16:15-20). This is why we can say that Paul healed them because operating and flowing in the supernatural just became natural to him.

Look at the last verse: *"And they went forth, and preached everywhere, the Lord working with them, and confirming the word with signs following. Amen"* (Mark 16:20).

The word "sign" is the Greek word "semeion," and

the Greek word "semaino." Both words together mean "to make a mark." An indication, miracle, sign, token or wonder.

God is about to move on His people in such a way that He will leave His mark everywhere that their feet tread, and their voices are heard. After all, it is God that sends his apostles, prophets, pastors, teachers, and evangelists. The word "apostle" or "apostolic" means "sent one." God is about to leave an indication that one of His prophets was here, where there will be a mighty work of the miraculous with supernatural signs and wonders following. God will make us a sign, a token, and a wonder.

"I am the true vine, and my Father is the husbandman. Every branch in me that beareth not fruit he taketh away: and every branch that beareth fruit, he purgeth it, that it may bring forth more fruit. Now ye are clean through the word which I have spoken unto you. Abide in me, and I in you. As the branch cannot bear fruit of itself, except it abide in the vine; no more can ye, except ye abide in me. I am the vine, ye are the branches: He that abideth in me, and I in him, the same bringeth forth much fruit: for without me ye can do nothing" (John 15:1-5).

It is vitally important for each and every one of us that is a believer to stay connected to the vine, Jesus Christ. If we do, He promises to cleanse, purge, and use us. He will help us to bring forth much fruit. Remember, we shall be like trees planted by rivers of living water, that bringeth forth his fruit in his season, and our leaf shall not wither, and whatsoever we doeth shall prosper. (Read Psalm 1). Stay connected for it is by this connection to Jesus Christ, that we will find the power, the ability, and the greatness in our own selves that will make way for us to succeed here in the Earth. Remember your gift will make room for you; therefore, your gifts only can be found in and through Christ Jesus, the true vine.

Stay connected and watch the power and glory of God overtake your life with supernatural signs and wonders following.

Now we are ready, for what's to come!!!

I encourage you that if you have never received Jesus Christ as your personal Savior, and you desire to do so, repeat this prayer after me:
Dear Heavenly Father, I know that I am a sinner. I have sinned against you and against the laws of your Word. Save me, God. Come into my heart, cleanse me, fill me, mold me, shape me, and use me in any way you see fit. Satan I renounce you; you are not my God. Now shut up and come out in the name of Jesus. I remind myself now that whom the Son sets free is free indeed. In Jesus Name, amen and amen.

You now will be given instructions by God as to what to do next with your life as you humbly submit it unto Him.

If you desire to receive the baptism of the Holy Spirit with evidence of speaking in tongues, then repeat this prayer after me:
Heavenly Father, I thank you that I am saved by your grace. Now I receive the full immersion, the baptism of the Holy Spirit. Fill me, dwell in me, immerse me, overtake me, and overflow inside of the wells of my mind, heart, life, and spirit. Overtake my tongue Lord God; loose my tongue to speak in your Heavenly language, as I submit to you as well. Out of my belly shall rivers of living water flow; now let the river flow. In Jesus Name, I pray, and I receive. In Jesus Name, amen and amen.

If you have prayed any of these prayers, we encourage you to leave us an email at: revivalfireapostolicministries@gmail.com or visit us on the web at revivalfireapostolic.org

In Christ Service, God Bless.

Tim Ranyak

www.ingramcontent.com/pod-product-compliance
Lightning Source LLC
Chambersburg PA
CBHW060406050426
42449CB00009B/1923